TITANIC

Based on an account from
Disaster at Sea by John Marriott

Retold by Diana Birkbeck

A Birkbeck Oxford Series

Heinemann Educational Publishers
Halley Court, Jordan Hill, Oxford OX2 8EJ
A division of Reed Educational and Professional Publishing Ltd

OXFORD MELBOURNE AUCKLAND
JOHANNESBURG BLANTYRE GABORONE
IBADAN PORTSMOUTH (NH) USA CHICAGO

03 02
10 9 8 7 6 5 4 3

ISBN 0 435 10446 2

Designed and produced by Artistix
Illustrations by Mike Taylor
Cover design by Artistix
The photo on page 3 is reproduced courtesy of Corbis UK Ltd
Printed and bound in the UK by Thomson Litho Ltd

Tel: 01865 888058 email: info.he@heinemann.co.uk

'She's the safest ship ever built,' said the Chief Designer as he discussed the great new ocean liner, *Titanic*, with her Captain. At 41,000 tons, she was so big and so high that no sea could wash over her. Three days later, on 15 April 1912, on her maiden voyage, *Titanic* sank after hitting an iceberg. Out of 2,235 people on board, 1,522 were lost.

She was bound for New York. Amongst the first-class passengers was a large number of rich and famous people. There were actors and actresses and at least ten millionaires on board.

Titanic took the great circle route to New York that all liners used. This route was outside the normal limit of the ice, but went through a part marked on the sea-chart: 'Icebergs have been seen within this line in April, May and June.'

It was four days into the trip and the passengers were living it up. In the evening, the scene in first-class was like a film set. There were men and women in beautiful clothes, drinking, dining and dancing to live bands.

The weather had been fine, but on the evening of Sunday 14 April it suddenly felt colder. When there are icebergs in the water, it chills the air. Few of the passengers knew this and they went on happily drinking their cocktails. But the Captain knew what the cold weather meant and he ordered the men in the crow's nest to keep a good look-out for icebergs. He did not, however, think the danger so great that the ship should slow down.

All seemed well until about 11 o'clock, when there was one stroke of a gong. It was the danger signal from the crow's nest and meant, 'object right ahead'. It was followed by a telephone call to the First Officer saying, 'Iceberg right ahead'. The First Officer saw a huge iceberg. At once he ordered the ship to be steered to the left. Slowly, the ship began to turn. For a moment it looked as if she had missed the iceberg. But it was too late – she was going too fast, and she struck the iceberg on her right side.

On board, all that was felt was a small bump. But the iceberg went well below the water and the damage to the ship could not be seen at first.

The Captain was woken up and told what had happened. At first, he was not too concerned as ships had hit icebergs before and had survived. He sent for the Chief Designer and they went below to inspect the damage.

Titanic was filling up with water. The firemen in the boiler room reported that the whole of the right side of the ship seemed to have caved in. The iceberg must have cut a great gash all along the side.

The Chief Designer then gave the Captain his verdict. As soon as one boiler room was full, the water would spill over into the next and then the next until the ship sank. They had one and a half hours before she went down.

The Captain ordered the lifeboats to be got ready. He then told the men in the wireless room to start sending out distress signals. The call was heard by a number of ships, one of which was only fifty-eight miles away. This ship set off at once to help *Titanic*.

At first, most of the passengers did not realize what was happening and went on merrily drinking and dancing. Then they heard a shout, 'All passengers on deck with life-belts on!' It was midnight.

At 12.20 a.m., the order was given to lower the lifeboats. Women and children were to go first. They were very slow to get into the boats as they felt safer on the ship, so the first boats entered the water only half full. The last boat left the ship at 2.05 a.m., only fifteen minutes before the ship finally sank.

Many of the third-class passengers had not even found their way up to the deck. Then they all rushed up on to the boat deck – but it was too late, the last boat had left! There were 1,500 people still on board.

The band played on bravely as the ship sank under them. All the bandsmen were drowned.

The water was rising fast. As *Titanic's* bows dipped lower and lower, the great ship began to lift her stern, until she was standing on her nose in the water. A few minutes later, some explosions were heard. She began to sink further into the sea and at 2.20 a.m. she disappeared under the water. All the people on deck were washed into the sea.

The sea was icy and many people died quickly from the cold, though some were still alive and shouting for help. Seven lifeboats did manage to pick up a few of them, but the people in the other boats refused to turn back to save those in the sea. The cries of those in the water slowly became quiet as one after another died from the cold.

At 4 a.m. the first rescue ship arrived, one hour forty minutes after *Titanic* had sunk. At first, the lifeboats could not be seen because it was too dark, but as day came they were picked up. No survivors were found in the sea, only dead bodies. Most of the dead were third-class passengers.

Titanic was one of the worst sea disasters in peace-time the world has ever known. It should never have happened. Although the Captain went down with his ship, much of the blame was his. He should have taken more care. He knew that there were icebergs about, but he did not put extra men on the look-out, nor did he warn the passengers. When the iceberg was seen, he did not reduce speed.

There were too few lifeboats. Even if they had all left full, there was room for only 1,178 people in them. That left the rest to drown.

Lessons were learnt from the disaster of *Titanic*. But it was too late for the 1,522 people who had lost their lives.

Word list

This story is suitable for use when pupils have reached page 169 of the *Alpha to Omega Handbook*.

There are a number of words in the story that are taught beyond page 169 of the *Alpha to Omega Handbook*. Those that students may find difficult to *read* are included in the 'Harder words' list below.

Words and phrases special to the story
1   Chief De/sign/er
2   *Titanic*
3   iceberg
4   New York

Harder words
1   ocean
2   Captain
3   April
4   people
5   pass/en/gers
6   actors
7   act/ress/es
8   mill/ion/aires
9   e/ven/ing
10   scene
11   moment
12   realize
13   minutes
14   ex/plo/sions
15   quiet
16   dis/as/ter
17   extra